Instructor's Manual
to accompany

Introduction to Rhetorical Theory

Second Edition

Gerard A. Hauser

prepared by
Amy Grim
University of Colorado

WAVELAND PRESS, INC.

Prospect Heights, Illinois

For information about this book, contact:
Waveland Press, Inc.
P.O. Box 400
Prospect Heights, Illinois 60070
(847) 634-0081
www.waveland.com

Contents

Introduction

"This class lives and dies by examples." From my very first meeting with Dr. Hauser as his teaching assistant through the writing of this manual, this mantra has been foremost in my mind as a teacher of rhetoric. We have found that one of the best ways to bring rhetorical theory to life for undergraduates is to have them generate many of the examples themselves. To that end, the "City as Text" case study and many of the discussion prompts for each chapter suggest ways to engage students in this inventional aspect of the course.

I have designed this manual to be heuristic rather than prescriptive. My hope is that the materials are flexible enough to allow instructors to adapt them for their own unique courses, while providing enough of a foundation so that they don't have to do everything from scratch. Each chapter includes a review of key concepts, test items (true-false, multiple choice, matching, short answer), and several discussion prompts. The key concepts can easily be converted into fill-in-the-blank questions, and many of the discussion prompts can be revised as short paper and essay exam topics. These prompts also include ideas for selecting exemplar texts for each chapter, and teachers undoubtedly will want to select additional materials more suited to their classes. Several good speech anthologies, clippings from popular media, a few hours of web browsing, and a ready hand on the record button will complement the book and this manual immeasurably.

Finally, this is a collaborative work. Many of the questions and ideas are culled from or inspired by items used by Dr. Hauser and his teaching assistants at the University of Colorado. I am greatly indebted to them for providing the raw materials and creative inspiration for this manual.

Term Project
"City as Text" Case Study

The "City as Text" case study is designed to give students a concrete understanding of how rhetoric constitutes the world in which we live. Through an extended research project of a current local issue, students can learn to recognize and apply rhetorical theories and concepts outside of the classroom, and they can learn how to participate in local civic life.

The central idea is to investigate the city in terms of a current local issue. Throughout the semester, students complete various small assignments that are designed to help them identify, describe, and analyze a local public problem from a rhetorical point of view. Using a single issue for multiple assignments allows students to experiment with different theoretical lenses and to come to a deeper understanding of the issue. In short, the "City as Text" assignment asks students to apply the wide range of theory presented in the course to a particular case.

"City as Text" is suitable as either an individual or a group project and is quite flexible. In addition to providing good writing opportunities, the projects are an excellent way to encourage class discussion. Once students become familiar with their cases, they are often eager to talk about their issue in class. Each chapter in this manual includes discussion prompts specifically geared to the case study. Teachers may want to use these as homework assignments, short paper topics, discussion starters, or in-class activities. In addition, the case study can be an excellent way to incorporate service learning into the course.

Although most students will know how to do library or electronic research for a term paper, many may be unfamiliar with the basic field research techniques needed for this project. Depending on the course, teachers may need to spend some time discussing basic ethnographic techniques including collecting primary texts, participant observation, writing field notes, interviewing, and the like.

Ideas for Assignments

Case File. As students gather information about their issue, it may be helpful to have them develop and maintain a case file consisting of media clippings, a who's who of the major participants, a chronology of how the issue has developed to date, identification of specific points of controversy, etc.

Field Research Log. Ask students to keep a running journal of notes of meetings, informal interaction, vernacular rhetoric, material culture, leads, and ideas related to the project. The log can consist of informal notes as well as specific homework assignments (e.g., list the different groups vying for ownership of the issue, write a paragraph explaining how pathos is invoked, unpack an enthymeme associated with the issue).

Observation Reports. Several times throughout the semester, ask students to attend a meeting or public event associated with the issue and to write up a *description* of it. Material from these reports can be incorporated into subsequent analysis papers.

Analysis Papers. Apply a theory or set of concepts to some aspect of the issue. See the case study discussion prompts in this manual for specific suggestions.

Interviews. Have students conduct information-gathering interviews with the leading advocates of the issue. In addition, "person-on-the-street" interviews can be used to get a sense of the vernacular public opinion about the issue.

Homework Assignments. Ask students to bring in examples of various texts to use throughout the course. Collect pamphlets and flyers, editorials, news reports, etc., suitable for in-class analysis and discussion.

Annotated Bibliographies. Ask students to consult the scholarly literature about the issue (e.g., has this kind of community dispute been studied systematically?) and/or the theoretical perspective(s) they may wish to employ in the final paper (e.g., taking narrative as the primary analytic lens, what have scholars written about narrative in public discourse?).

Final Term Paper. Ask students to synthesize what they have learned by writing a detailed critical analysis of the issue using one or several of the theories discussed in class. The paper could draw from scholarly literature and/or field research to provide specific evidence for claims.

Advocacy Statement. After having spent the entire semester on the issue, ask students to weigh in on the issue—to create rhetoric that takes a position on the issue and that is designed to engage the public discussion. This could take the form of a letter to the editor, an op-ed essay, a position paper, or a speech or presentation to a local group. As a complement, students can reflect and write about the strategic rhetorical choices they made while crafting the advocacy statement for a particular audience.

1

The Eventfulness
of Rhetoric

Key Concepts

- The study of **human communication** is concerned with what happens when at least one person engages at least one other person in an act of shared meaning and interpretation through the use of symbols.

- **Rhetoric**, as one form of communication, is specifically concerned with the use of symbols to induce social action. Rhetoric is goal-oriented, pragmatic, and seeks to influence human choices about specific situations.

- Communication can be viewed as a **process** or an **event. Processes** are characterized by continuous sequential developments that involve changes, whereas **events** occur at a specific time and place. While rhetoric can be investigated in terms of process, it is essentially manifested as an event addressed to a particular situation.

- Our experience of the world is marked by both **continuity** (sequential development) and **discontinuity** (breaks in the sequence). Discontinuities invite rhetorical communication.

- Rhetorical events take place in the realm of **action**—the social world where human choice is involved.

- **Event types** are modes of action. They consist of the general characteristics that distinguish one group of events from another. Event types include: **situated action, symbolic action, transaction, social action, strategic action**, and **constitutive action**.

4

- Rhetoric is a **practical art**. It concerns matters where humans must make choices about how to conduct their affairs. Typically, these are matters where there is no consensus of opinion and no certain course of action to follow. Rhetoric is an art because it deals with uncertainty.
- **Rhetorical theory** focuses on the use of symbolic forms, especially persuasive appeals, to promote social action and coordination.
- Rhetoric is both a **method** and a **practice**. As **method**, rhetoric prescribes certain principles in the construction of communicative appeals. As **practice**, rhetoric is a communicative performance designed to influence practical choices.

♫

Test Items

True or False

1. Rhetoric is best defined as propaganda. (F)
2. Nonverbal communication falls outside the scope of rhetoric. (F)
3. Communication is not a thing. (T)
4. Events consist of sequential developments that change over time. (F)
5. Rhetoric typically thrives in the discontinuities of experience. (T)

Multiple Choice

1. Rhetoric is primarily concerned with:
   a. managing symbols to influence conduct
   b. investigating continuities of experience
   c. conveying information
   d. unintentional communication

2. Rhetoric can be characterized as all of the following *except*:
   a. a method
   b. an art
   c. a social practice
   d. an attitude

3. Rhetoric is best suited to situations in which outcomes are:
   a. public
   b. predictable
   c. uncertain
   d. important

4. As a rhetorical construction, a presidential campaign can be considered a(n) _____, whereas a specific debate is a(n) _____.

a. thing, event

b. event, process

c. thing, process

d. process, event

5. An event type is:

a. a type of motion

b. a typical mode of action

c. a specific manifestation of language use at a specific time

d. a dynamic exchange of symbols between persons

Matching

1. social action (d)

2. symbolic action (a)

3. constitutive action (e)

4. strategic action (f)

5. situated action (b)

a. uniting and dividing from each other based on the way we talk about things

b. addressed to somebody specific and is contingent on the dynamics of a given case

c. developing sequential relations to explain a particular situation

d. constructing mutually compatible interpretations of a given situation

e. constructing situational truths that give meaning to social behavior

f. deliberate communication designed to achieve a particular goal

Short Answer

Define and provide an example of each of the following terms.

1. communication

2. rhetoric

3. rhetorical events

4. rhetorical processes

5. rhetoric as a practical art

Discussion Prompts

- Ask students to solicit colloquial definitions of rhetoric from friends, coworkers, family, or acquaintances. Share with the class. What are the themes that emerge from these common understandings of rhetoric? Is rhetoric generally understood as a "good" or "bad" form of communication? Why? How does Hauser's definition of rhetoric depart from these common views?

- What distinguishes rhetoric from other forms of communication? What are some situations in which you might engage in rhetoric as opposed to other types of communication?

- Describe a political campaign for elected office (or a social movement, college course, public relations campaign) in terms of process. What specific events comprise this process? What kinds of questions arise when we think of this communication activity in terms of process? What kinds of questions arise when we think of it in terms of events?

- Hauser claims that discontinuity of experience is the soil in which rhetoric grows. What does he mean by this? Why is rhetoric particularly suited for addressing discontinuities, or breaks, in the normal course of affairs? Have you witnessed or experienced a discontinuity that called for some kind of rhetorical response? What was it? What was the response? Was the response appropriate to the situation? Does rhetoric play a role in maintaining the continuity of experience?

- Hauser writes that rhetoric, no matter how intelligently executed, does not guarantee a favorable outcome. Why not?

- Students need to begin thinking about possible topics for their semester projects. Ask them to identify some current discontinuities in their communities that are calling for some sort of response. What are the pending issues in the community? How do these issues represent a break from the normal course of affairs? Who is addressing the situation through rhetoric?

🌮 2 🍋

Rhetorical Thinking

🌮
Key Concepts

- Rhetorical communication can be thought of as a discursive method for thinking through public problems or as a means to achieve predetermined ends. Rhetorical communication, then, can be used to foster or inhibit participatory processes.

- Aristotle taught that rhetoric was both a **practical art** (a mode of action with consequences in the world) and a **productive art** (a mode of thinking that produced judgment).

- **Social practices** refer to modes of conduct that are constitutive of an act. Social practices can be formal or informal, are culturally specific, and assume a relationship between those who engage in the practice and the rest of society.

- In antiquity, rhetoric as a social practice emerged in relation to other communicative social practices: **narrative** and **dialectic**.

- **Narratives** are stories that express the conventional wisdom, norms, and values of a culture. They tend not to be reflective, or critical, of societal norms. Narratives encourage members of a society to act in particular ways.

- **Dialectic** is a question and answer method designed to examine critically the strength or truthfulness of an idea. Truthful propositions can withstand critical examination. Dialectic aims at certainty, but not necessarily action.

- **Rhetoric** is a mode of two-sided argument designed to provide guidance for belief and conduct in a particular case. It is suited for open-

8

ended, or contingent, matters in which there are no certain answers. It uses appeals suited to a particular audience.

- Sophistic rhetoric was based on the idea of arguing from **probability.** The method they used was called **dissoi logoi**, or two-sided argument.

- For the Sophists, sound rhetorical practice was characterized as having **prepon** (propriety); it was specific to a specific time, place, and audience. **Kairos** is the idea that rhetors should be on the alert for opportune moments to make specific arguments.

- As a **method**, rhetoric involves the purposive selection and arrangement of symbols in order to manage a particular situation. Rhetoric's basic concern is with how party A (a rhetor) speaks or writes to party B (an audience) to affect that person's choices.

- Aristotle claimed that **rhetoric and dialectic are counterparts**, or complementary modes of communication. Both are modes of arguing. Both are universal methods having no subject matter of their own. Both are based on opinion and can yield only probable solutions. They differ with respect to outcome: the end of dialectic is criticism, while the end of rhetoric is persuasion.

ഹ
Test Items

True or False

1. Dialectic is the Sophistic method of the two-sided argument. (F)
2. Aristotle claimed that rhetoric and dialectic are opposites. (F)
3. Social practices are culturally specific. (T)
4. Narratives tend to challenge societal norms. (F)
5. Plato believed that there are universal truths and that words can fully capture them. (F)

Multiple Choice

1. Rhetoric and dialectic share all of the following traits *except*:

   a. both have no subject matter of their own

   b. both are modes of arguing

   c. **both examine opinions and the necessary claims that must follow**

   d. both begin with opinions

2. A sense of kairos means:

   a. knowing when to speak and when to be silent

   b. making an argument regardless of present circumstances

   c. being able to see a proposition from different points of view

   d. knowing how to experiment with lang.age to achieve desired ends

3. A debate among scientists about the causes of global warming most closely approximates which communicative practice?

   a. narrative

   b. dialectic

   c. rhetoric

   d. diagnostic

4. Narratives are:

   a. only employed by poets and fiction writers

   b. unreliable sources of cultural values

   c. direct prescriptions for action

   d. means of conveying cultural norms and traditions

5. Sophistic rhetoric was based on the idea of argument from:

   a. propriety

   b. probability

   c. perspective

   d. logical consistency

Matching

1. Plato (d)

2. Gorgias (b)

3. Protagoras (a)

4. Aristotle (e)

5. Socrates (c)

a. "Man is the measure of all things."

b. "Reality does not exist. If reality exists, it cannot be grasped. If reality could be grasped, it could not be communicated."

c. Developed a question-and-answer method for arriving at truth.

d. By questioning the opinions of the day, we can expose which ones are false.

e. "Rhetoric is the counterpart of dialectic."

f. "Rhetoric is the art of effective expression."

Short Answer

Define and provide an example of each of the following terms.

1. narrative
2. dialectic
3. rhetoric
4. kairos
5. dissoi logoi

ᔡ
Discussion Prompts

- Compare and contrast rhetorical communication as a way of thinking through social problems versus as a means to achieve predetermined ends. What are the consequences of thinking about rhetoric in each of these ways? How do these relate to the two central themes of this chapter: rhetoric as a social practice and rhetoric as a method?

- Ask students to think of two communicative exchanges they have experienced, one in which the purpose was to think through an idea and one in which a participant was tying to persuade another toward his or her own agenda. What sorts of communicative acts characterized each interaction? How did the participants act and react in each circumstance? Would the outcome have been different if the alternative approach were used?

- Compare and contrast narrative, dialectic, and rhetoric (figure 2.1 is a helpful summary). How does each contribute to public decision making? Is one form superior to another for arriving at public judgments?

- Ask students to write or perform a dialectic, starting with a proposition and systematically examining its assumptions through the question and answer method. Consider starting with the following quote: "'Beauty is truth, truth beauty,'—that is all Ye know on earth, and all Ye need to know" (John Keats, *Ode on a Grecian Urn*, 1819).

- Ask students to consider a particular political issue (e.g., military action, euthanasia, legalization of drugs, gun control, etc.). How might narratives be used to construct this issue? Dialectic? Rhetoric?

- Would Plato take issue with narrative and rhetoric as means of arriving at judgments? What would be his particular criticisms of each method? How would the Sophists react to Plato's charges and defend their own method? How would epic poets (i.e., storytellers) react to Plato's charges and defend their own method? If your students, are game, consider role-playing.

- This chapter provides a good opportunity to introduce students to primary ancient texts on rhetoric. Have students read relevant excerpts from Plato's *Phaedrus* and Gorgias's *Encomium of Helen*. In class, divide the students into teams where they debate Plato's versus Gorgias's perspectives, then have them switch sides to argue the opposite case (thereby demonstrating the practice of dissoi logoi, or the two-sided argument).

• Aristotle claimed that rhetoric and dialectic are counterparts, or complementary forms of communication. How are they complementary? What is each best suited for? Is narrative similarly a counterpart to rhetoric and dialectic? Why/why not?

• For the case study, ask students to find examples of the various methods (narrative, dialectic, and rhetoric) in use. Examples might include a debate, a city council meeting, letters to the editor, op-ed essays, informal conversations, heated discussions, a dialogue among experts, etc. In your case, are the methods used in isolation, or are there instances where hybrids or mixed forms appear?

❦ 3 ❧

Rhetorical Opportunities

❦
Key Concepts

- Humans act on the basis of how they define **situations**.
- The meanings of situations emerge and are relative. **Emergence** refers to the meaning of an event across time. **Relativity** refers to the meaning of an event based on the perspective of the individual.
- **Rhetorical situations** are ones in which discourse can partially or completely resolve the problem at hand. A rhetorical situation calls for a communicative response.
- According to Bitzer, every rhetorical situation is composed of an **exigence**, an **audience**, and **constraints**.
- An **exigence** is "an imperfection marked by urgency," a defect (or discontinuity) that can be resolved through communication. Rhetorical situations can have multiple exigencies, though one may be the **controlling exigence**.
- **Audiences** consist only of those individuals who are capable of being influenced and who are capable of mediating change. Audiences are not preexisting groups with a fixed identity. Rather, they are called into existence by rhetoric.
- **Constraints** are both the limitations and opportunities present in a situation that influence what may or may not be said. Constraints may be physical or psychological and bear on both the speaker and the audience.

13

- Rhetorical situations are dynamic—they change over time. The life cycle of a rhetorical situation passes through four stages: **origin, maturity, deterioration,** and **disintegration**.

- Ideally, a rhetorical situation will evoke a **fitting response**, one that is appropriate and responsive to the exigence. A fitting response is not necessarily a successful one, but one that is addressed to resolving the complex of factors that define the situation. Fitting responses are influenced by the life-cycle stage of the situation and, in turn, will influence how the life cycle develops.

- A rhetorical situation is not deterministic (i.e., the discourse is totally shaped by contextual elements that are beyond the rhetor's control). A **rhetor's intentions** play a significant role in shaping and resolving dynamic situations.

♋

Test Items

True or False

1. A rhetorical situation can have multiple exigencies. (T)
2. A fitting response is a successful response. (F)
3. Meanings emerge and are relative. (T)
4. Constraints refer to situational limitations that preclude what may be said. (F)
5. A rhetor's intentions help to shape the demands of a situation. (T)

Multiple Choice

1. Emergence refers to:
   a. how the meaning of a rhetorical situation is defined by its origin
   b. the absence of a static standpoint from which to view a situation
   c. how meanings of situations change over time
   d. an imperfection marked by urgency

2. Relativity refers to:
   a. how the meaning of a situation is based on the perspective of the individual
   b. how the success of a rhetorical appeal depends on the life cycle of a situation
   c. how meanings develop in relation to their contexts
   d. how rhetoric adjusts people to ideas and ideas to people

3. Which of the following statements characterizes an audience?
   a. people who have a vested interest in the outcome and are capable of mediating change
   b. people who pre-exist the rhetorical event and are waiting to hear the rhetor's appeals
   c. people who are recipients of a rhetorical appeal
   d. people who are capable of being influenced and who can mediate change

4. All of the following characterize the life cycle of a rhetorical situation *except*:
   a. stages may be shortened or lengthened as new dimensions of the situation are perceived
   b. a fitting response brings an end to the life cycle of the situation
   c. stages influence what can be considered a fitting response
   d. responses influence how the situation proceeds through the stages

5. Constraints are:
   a. objective assessments of a given situation
   b. determined by the results of natural forces
   c. physical and psychological limitations and opportunities of a given situation
   d. restrictions on freedom of speech in a given situation

Matching

Students are protesting on the steps of the main building on campus. They are calling for the university to cancel its contract with an athletic shoe company that manufactures its wares in sweatshops. The protest is drawing a large crowd. Protestors are asking that students boycott all college sporting events until the university adopts the proposed course of action.

1. exigence (c)

2. rhetorical audience (d)

3. non-rhetorical audience (e)

4. physical constraints (b)

5. psychological constraints (a)

a. The protestors realize that getting students to boycott all sporting events is a difficult proposition; after all, they receive discounted tickets and sweatshops are remote from their daily concerns.

b. The protesters plan their protest for the noon hour, when they know lots of students will be on campus.

c. The university has a long-term contract with an athletic shoe company. Recent news reports have revealed that the company uses sweatshops to manufacture its goods.

d. College students on this campus are generally thought to be socially responsible. If they boycotted the games, the university administration would surely take notice.

e. The protest receives national news coverage. Students from other campuses agree that the contract should be terminated.

f. The university issues a statement that it intends to honor its contract.

Short Answer

Define and provide an example of each of the following terms.

1. exigence
2. origin
3. maturity
4. deterioration
5. disintegration

ॐ

Discussion Prompts

- Ask students to think of an event or turning point in their life in which the meaning of that event changed over time. How did you originally interpret the event? How do you interpret that event now? What has influenced your change in perspective? Reconsider the situation from the perspective of someone else in your life. How did that person originally interpret the event? Has their interpretation also changed over time? How do your experiences illustrate that *meanings emerge and are relative* and that *humans act on the basis of how they define a situation*?

- Bitzer claims that rhetorical exigencies are "imperfections marked by urgency." How does this relate to the concept of discontinuity introduced in chapter one?

- Ask students to brainstorm recurrent types of rhetorical situations (war speeches, crisis rhetoric, apologia, eulogies, etc.). What makes these situations *rhetorical*? How can communication resolve or partially resolve these recurrent situations?

- Neighborhoods near campus are experiencing a crime wave, with incidents ranging from vandalism and petty theft to harassment and assault. How might different interested groups define the situation (e.g., students, student residents of the neighborhood, non-student residents of the neighborhood, parents, police, the university administration)? How might these different definitions influence appropriate action? Is this a rhetorical situation, as Bitzer defines it? If so, identify exigence(s), audience(s), and constraints.

- Can the attacks on the World Trade Center and the Pentagon be considered exigencies of a rhetorical situation? Why or why not? What kind of rhetorical response was engendered by the situation? View or read the text of President Bush's remarks upon arrival at Barksdale Air Force Base on the evening of September 11, 2001. Identify the constituent elements of the rhetorical situation. Did the president deliver a fitting response?

- View or read the text of Robert F. Kennedy's address following the assassination Martin Luther King Jr. on April 4, 1968. (Be sure to provide enough background information so that students may be able to assess the situation.) What rhetorical situation were Kennedy and his audience expecting that evening? How and why did that situation change? If Kennedy had chosen to give his stump campaign speech, would it have been a fitting response? What constraints confronted the speaker and audience? Was his audience capable of mediating the change he calls for in his speech? Was this speech a fitting response to the situation? Why? Kennedy was himself assassinated three months after delivering this speech. Does that change the meaning of this rhetorical event?

- Ask students to attend a speaking event related to their case study. Identify the different elements of the rhetorical situation. What is the exigence that prompted the event? Who is the audience? Are there several audiences or just one? Is the audience capable of being influenced? What are the physical and psychological constraints? Does the event constitute a fitting response to the exigence? Why or why not? What might the speaker(s) have done differently to craft a more fitting response? What phase of the life cycle characterizes this situation? How does the life cycle influence the types of appeals that can be made?

ᘒ 4 ᘕ

Making Commitments through Rhetoric

ᘒ
Key Concepts

- Rhetors not only act as change agents in the world; rhetors themselves can be transformed through rhetoric. Every rhetorical transaction involves personal stakes for all participants.

- Rhetoric makes **commitments**. What we say and how we say it reflects our choices and commitments we have made to ourselves, to others, to our ideas, and to the world in which we live.

- Rhetoric is **other-directed** communication. It is a mode of discourse addressed to others in order to influence their thinking or conduct.

- **Expressive communication** is self-directed discourse that states our feelings about something. It is not primarily intended to change thought or conduct, though expressive communication can also serve rhetorical ends.

- **Arguments** consist of reasons supported by data that lead to a specific conclusion. Arguments are not measured merely by their acceptability to listeners, but by their ability to withstand refutation and rebuttal.

- Johnstone gives three conditions for **genuine argument**:

  1. We must assume that the audience is beyond our control. We must respect their freedom of choice.

2. The audience is free to ignore, disbelieve, or refute our arguments. Arguments run the risk of being defeated.

3. Both the arguer and those responding have an interest in the outcome. All those involved have a stake in the consequences.

- Arguments force us to consider alternative or contradictory views and impulses, thereby helping us to become self-aware of our own beliefs, values, and commitments.

- A **bilateral argument** is guided by the principle that we can only use types of appeals that we would permit our interlocutors to use; all participants are entitled to transmit messages in the same way. Bilateral communication can form a wedge whereby we become aware of our stake in a rhetorical situation. A **wedge** is the separation of the rhetor from the message thereby allowing us to consider that the message may have to be revised.

- A **unilateral argument** is one in which the arguer uses types of appeals that are not available to interlocutors. Unilateral argument denies participants equal opportunity of response.

- Rhetoric can **reflect a self**. We can form impressions of a rhetor through her typical manner of reasoning and language use. Patterns of argument (such as **definition**, **similitude**, and **cause and effect**) reflect a communicator's vision of the world.

- Rhetoric can **evoke a self**. By forcing individuals to reexamine their assumptions, rhetoric can influence one to reconsider or discover a new self. It can bring us to a new self-awareness.

- Rhetoric can **maintain a self**. It can support and sustain self-identity.

- Rhetoric can **destroy a self**. It can be used to scapegoat a particular group and symbolically "kill" its target, or undermine its identity.

☙

Test Items

True or False

1. Rhetorical communication, like all communication, is other-directed. (F)

2. Rhetoric involves self-risk. (T)

3. An argument refers to a communicative exchange in which people disagree. (F)

4. Bilateral arguments conform to the golden rule. (T)

5. Unilateral communication relies on intimidation tactics. (F)

Multiple Choice

1. "Art for art's sake" characterizes which form of communication?

   a. rhetorical communication

   b. interpersonal communication

   c. bilateral communication

   d. expressive communication

2. According to Johnstone, genuine arguments meet all of the following conditions *except*:

   a. all parties have equal opportunity to respond

   b. the audience is free to refute arguments

   c. all participants have an interest in the outcome

   d. the audience is not regarded as an object of manipulation

3. One could infer that individuals who typically make arguments by definition:

   a. respect their audience's ability to be self-reflective

   b. believe that there are "truths" and that our conduct should be guided by them

   c. are seeking an immediate response

   d. believe that different situations demand different courses of action

4. Bilateral communication is guided by the principle that:

   a. the arguer must use no device of argument that she could not in principle permit her interlocutor to use

   b. the arguer must use no device of argument that she could not support with evidence

   c. the arguer must be able to argue both sides of an issue

   d. the arguer may use deception only if her intentions are honorable

5. Arguments by cause and effect:

   a. emphasize the relationships between different situations

   b. emphasize the contingency of a situation

   c. emphasize the essential characteristics of a situation

   d. emphasize the developmental features of a situation

Matching

1. scapegoating (e)
2. rhetorical communication (d)
3. expressive communication (f)
4. unilateral communication (a)
5. bilateral communication (c)

a. "This is my house. These are my rules, period."

b. "Read my lips: No new taxes!"

c. "I know you have a lot of other commitments at the moment, but I'm asking you to make this class a higher priority."

d. "Let's see if we can come to an agreement on this. We need to make a decision about what to do next."

e. "People who burn the flag are unpatriotic traitors who symbolize all that is wrong with our country."

f. "Dear Diary: Today I faced one of my biggest fears . . ."

Short Answer

Define and provide an example of each of the following statements.

1. Rhetoric can reflect a self.
2. Rhetoric can evoke a self.
3. Rhetoric can maintain a self.
4. Rhetoric can destroy a self.

 formatting

Discussion Prompts

- Ask students to think of instances in which they personally experienced unilateral and bilateral communication. How are you able to identify communication as either unilateral or bilateral? What kinds of cues helped you make this determination? What are the consequences of the different types of communication for you? Did you put yourself at risk? Did your conversational partner put him- or herself at risk? What were your impressions and feelings? How did you react to this type of communication? Would your reaction have been different if the other type of communication were used? Do people have to be equals to engage in bilateral communication?

- Ask students to watch (or view in class) a discussion-based television program. These might include an afternoon talk show, Sunday-morning news forum, a nighttime news program with several commentators from across the political spectrum, *Politically Incorrect*, a debate-type program, a roundtable discussion, etc. Identify examples of unilateral and bilateral communication. How are you able to identify whether it is unilateral or bilateral communication? What specific cues or lead you characterize the interaction as one form or the other? What are the consequences of each type of talk on these programs? What might the producers do to ensure that bilateral communication is encouraged? Should the producers do so? How would you convince them that this is a good thing to do?

- Charge students to plan a (fictional) campaign about campus safety. When might it be wise to engage in unilateral communication? What methods would you use? When might it be wise to engage in bilateral communication? What methods would you use? Does your campaign have any room for expressive communication? How might you encourage expressive communication?

- What does it mean to say rhetoric involves commitment and self-risk? What kinds of commitments do we make when we engage in rhetorical communication? How do we put ourselves at risk? Is risk limited to the notion that you might be challenged or discredited by others? How do we put our identity at risk when we engage in rhetoric?

- Many college campuses are visited by itinerant proselytizers. If your campus has one, have students spend half an hour observing the speaker, taking notes on the details of the interaction. Initiate a discussion of this rhetorical event in light of the concepts discussed in this chapter.

- By now students should be collecting quite a bit of data related to their case study. Ask them to examine news clippings, notes from interviews and meetings, field research notes, etc. and to select examples of unilateral and bilateral communication. For each example, identify the type of communication, the evidence from which they reached this conclusion, and the consequences of the type of communication for resolving the particular issue.

∾ 5 ∾

Public Judgment

∾
Key Concepts

- Rhetoric has a core civic concern with public decision making. Its **telos** (purpose) is judgment.

- A **public problem** is a matter of conflict and controversy that is (or should be) open to discussion in the arenas of public action by everyone with an interest in it. What we regard as a public problem is a rhetorical construction. Public problems are **agonistic** in character. Competing interests tend to vie for control of the problem.

- Gusfield identifies three features of public problems: **ownership**, **causal responsibility**, and **political responsibility**.

- **Ownership** refers to the ability to create and influence the public definition of a problem. As groups seek to control discussion and debate on the topic, they seek to become the **exclusive authority** on the problem, while diminishing the authority of opposing groups. Groups can also attempt to **disown** public problems by acts of word and deed that distance them from the problem and minimize their obligation.

- Owners seek to assign **responsibility** for a public problem. **Causal responsibility** refers to a shared belief about the sequence of occurrences that factually accounts for the existence of the problem. **Political responsibility** refers to claims that some office or group is obligated to do something about the problem.

- **Public consciousness** is shaped by **public performances** that call attention to a problem and by **cultural metaphors** that organize and orient public knowledge.

24

- **Publics theory** attempts to understand and critique how the rhetorical characteristics of public problems shape the publics that form around them and the opinions they form. Publics theory is both **descriptive** and **normative**.

- A **public** is that portion of the populace engaged in evolving shared opinion on a particular issue, with the intent of influencing its resolution. Developed societies consist of multiple publics. Publics are **active**. Publics **emerge** in rhetorical experience; they are not pre-given. Membership in a public requires **rhetorical competence**, or a capacity to participate in rhetorical experiences. Members of a public must exhibit such traits as: receptivity, critical listening, open-mindedness, active attempts to engage in bilateral communication, inventional skill, contingent thinking, and inclusivity.

- A **public sphere** is "a **discursive space** in which individuals and groups associate to discuss matters of mutual interest and, where possible, reach a common judgment about them. It is the site of rhetorically salient meanings." Democratic societies have multiple public spheres, formal (**institutional**) and informal (**preinstitutional**) discursive spaces where people communicate about public issues. **Counterpublic spheres** may develop if certain groups or interests are excluded from the dominant public sphere.

- Normative standards for assessing a particular public sphere include: the **publicity principle** (the right to make your views known), the **right to participate** in the public dialogue, **access to relevant information**, **access to relevant media of dissemination**, and **rights of free speech**.

- **Rhetorical ecology** refers to the conditions of a public sphere that may influence the full and open exchange of ideas. These conditions are **inclusion**, **range of appeals**, **believable appearance**, **rhetorically salient meaning**, **tolerance**, and **empowerment of its public**.

- As an alternative to opinion polls, rhetoricians understand **public opinion** as a discursive expression of civil judgment that reflects a common understanding among members of a public. Public opinion emerges from people deliberating the merits of ideas and actions. We can detect public opinion by surveilling **vernacular rhetoric**, or everyday interactions and communicative practices. When we observe vernacular rhetoric, we place more **weight** on the opinions of those who are actively engaged, we pay attention to the **intensity** of opinion, and notice that public opinion has **duration**, or persistence over time. Public opinion of this sort is not **doxa** (strongly held but weakly grounded preferences), but **public judgment**.

ℒ

Test Items

True or False

1. The four attributes of ownership are: control, exclusive authority, transferability, and potential loss. (T)

2. On any given issue, there can only be one public. (F)

3. A public sphere is a physical place in which individuals and groups assemble to discuss matters of mutual interest. (F)

4. Public opinion is a discursive expression of civil judgment. (T)

5. Once a group has established exclusive authority on a public problem, no other group can claim ownership. (F)

Multiple Choice

1. When competing groups try to control the discourse of a public problem, they are vying for:

   a. political responsibility

   b. causal responsibility

   c. ownership

   d. transference

2. A public's members must exhibit all of the following traits *except*:

   a. contingent thinking which opens all claims to amendment

   b. inclusivity of all relevant voices in the discussion

   c. receptivity to modes of expression in addition to argumentation

   d. active attempts to engage in unilateral communication

3. According to publics theory, a public

   a. consists of only those persons who are capable of being influenced by discourse and of being mediators of change

   b. is that portion of the population engaged in evolving shared opinion on a particular issue, with the intent of influencing its resolution

   c. is a fixed portion of the population that is capable of attending to the rhetorical situation

   d. has the ability to create and influence the public definition of a problem

4. After the Enron bankruptcy, many members of Congress returned (or gave to charity) campaign contributions from Enron. In doing so, these members of Congress were attempting to:

a. restrict access to the public sphere

b. affix causal responsibility for the scandal

c. become the exclusive authority on the problem

d. disown the problem

5. Assigning political responsibility for a public problem involves:

a. making claims about who or what caused the problem

b. surveilling vernacular rhetoric about the problem

c. identifying the portion of the populace engaged in forming opinions about the problem

d. asserting that a particular office or group is obligated to do something about the problem

Matching

1. institutional forums (c)

2. preinstitutional forums (d)

3. public sphere (f)

4. counterpublic sphere (e)

5. rhetorical ecology (a)

a. a set of conditions that influences the degree to which a public sphere accommodates full and open exchange of ideas

b. a set of standards we use to assess the rhetorical competence of publics

c. often have limited access and rules for speaking privileges and procedures

d. vernacular rhetoric

e. a discursive arena in which marginalized groups may deliberate public problems

f. arises to some degree whenever two or more people engage in serious discussion of a public issue

Short Answer

Define and provide an example of each of the following terms.

1. public problem

2. ownership

3. causal responsibility

4. political responsibility

5. public opinion

❧
Discussion Prompts

- How potential owners define a public problem greatly influences the course of public discussion about the problem, who is assigned responsibility for the problem, and potential resolutions. Ask students to think of a recent controversy on campus. What groups attempted to own the problem? What publics (and counterpublics) emerged? How did different groups define the problem? How did their definitions influence how they affixed causal and political responsibility for the problem? Did any group establish exclusive ownership of the problem? Was ownership transferred or lost at any time? What caused this shift in ownership? How did the public discussion influence the consideration of possible courses of action?

- Ask students to watch (or view in class) an investigative journalism report that includes interviews or statements from representatives of different groups who have an interest in a public problem. How did this problem emerge as a public problem? Who are the groups vying for ownership? How do they define the problem? How do they assign political and causal responsibility? Who is disowning the problem? Are the spokespersons exhibiting rhetorical competence? What publics emerge with this problem? Is anyone excluded from this public sphere? Would you expect a counterpublic sphere to develop?

- Compare and contrast a *public* as defined by publics theory and an *audience* as defined by the rhetorical situation theory. Are a public and an audience the same thing? How are they similar? How are they different? How does thinking about publics instead of audiences inform your understanding of rhetorical communication?

- Ask students to analyze a public forum (e.g., attend a city council meeting, watch roundtable discussion, read a transcript of a multiparty discussion about a public issue; *Harper's* magazine regularly publishes a "forum"). Evaluate this interaction in terms of one or more of the following: traits of rhetorical competence, normative standards for assessing public spheres, and traits of the rhetorical ecology of a public sphere.

- Select an issue that clearly illustrates the contestable nature of public and private problems, such as abortion, spousal abuse, gay rights, or sexual harassment. How do different owners define the problem as public or private? Whose interests do these definitions serve? How do they define indirect consequences of the problem? How do definitions of public and private delimit the boundaries of the public sphere in ways that disadvantage certain groups? What are the implications of these definitions for arriving at public judgment about the issue? Depending on the issue you choose, it may also be appropriate to discuss how counterpublic spheres develop and engage a dominant public sphere.

- Compare and contrast public opinion as measured by opinion polls and public opinion rhetorically construed as a discursive expression of civil judgment. What can we learn from each of these measures of public opinion? What kinds of information do they yield? What kinds of information do they exclude? Is one form superior to another for assessing public opinion? Are they complementary or competing perspectives? How might our elected representatives make use of both types of assessing public opinion?

- For the case study, have students identify the public problem, groups vying for ownership and disownership (and how they define the problem, assign responsibility, etc.), publics and counterpublics, the public spheres in which the problem is discussed (institutional and preinstitutional), and potential places to observe vernacular rhetoric about the problem. If appropriate, students may also perform analysis of the rhetoric of the public problem using the traits of rhetorical competence, the normative standards for assessing public spheres, and the traits of the rhetorical ecology of a public sphere.

∽ 6 ∾

Finding Ideas

∽
Key Concepts

- In rhetoric, the activity of finding things to say is called **invention**. **Invention** is the method of finding "sayables" (symbols) with the potential to transform some matter or question of an indeterminate nature into one that is determinate in the eyes of the audience. **Topical reasoning** is an inventional method used to generate fresh ideas suited to the rhetor, the topic, the audience, and the situation.

- **Creativity** is central to the inventional process. Each rhetorical transaction is a creative act. Through rhetorical interaction, people construct what they know, believe, and value about a common world. Creativity is necessary when standard interpretations and standard responses are not available, when solutions to problems are not ordinary or obvious.

- Problematic situations (in which the course of action is uncertain) are typically marked by some sort of tension: **conflict** (competing interests pull in opposite directions), **novelty** (new circumstances are outside our frame of reference), or **ambiguity** (meanings aren't clearly established). In each case, choices must be made. Our symbolic choices create meanings for the situation and provide **frames** for further analysis and interpretation.

- Invention is the branch of rhetoric concerned with discovering what might be communicated in a given situation. The **five canons** of classical rhetoric include **invention, disposition, style, memory,** and **delivery.**

- **Nomos** is the ancient Greek term for realities that are determined by human conventions.

- Topical thinking is akin to brainstorming. However, topical thinking uses a specific device to help generate ideas: a **topos**, or a "place" to find an argument. **Topoi** (or **commonplaces**) are **analytic**; they provide mental perspectives to help us explore a subject. Topoi are **contentless**; they can be applied to any particular subject. Topoi are **heuristic**; they help us generate new things to say about a subject.

- Aristotle identified three genres of speaking prevalent in ancient Greek public life. **Forensic** speeches, used in the law courts, were concerned with justice or injustice, guilt or innocence. **Deliberative** speeches, used in the legislative assembly, were concerned with expedience and inexpedience, advantage and injury. **Epideictic** speeches, given on ceremonial occasions, were concerned with praiseworthy or condemnable action, virtue and vice. Aristotle thought that a knowledge of the genres helped orators craft better appeals.

- There are three types of topical systems: common topics, specific topics, and review topics. **Konoi topoi** (common topics) apply to any subject matter and include the possible and impossible, past and future facts, and more and less magnitude. **Idia** (special or material topics) generate specific premises for a particular subject matter. **Review topics** also apply to any subject matter and include both attributes and relationships.

❧

Test Items

True or False

1. Invention refers to the eloquence of rhetoric. (F)
2. In phatic communication, form is more important than content. (T)
3. Konoi topoi supply specific premises for particular subjects. (F)
4. Forensic rhetoric concerns justice and injustice. (T)
5. Creativity is an act of symbolic expression. (T)

Multiple Choice

1. The five canons of rhetoric are
   a. invention, deliberation, style, memory, and delivery
   b. style, disposition, idia, eloquence, and memory
   c. delivery, style, invention, disposition, and memory
   d. invention, memory, elocution, deliberation, and delivery

2. Topoi refer to:
   a. ways to structure a speech
   b. places to find arguments
   c. stylistic devices
   d. all of the above

3. More and less, possible and impossible are:

   a. special topics
   b. idia
   c. review topics
   d. konoi topoi

4. The characteristics of topoi include:

   a. contentless, analytic, heuristic
   b. more and less, possible and impossible, past and future
   c. forensic, deliberative, epideictic
   d. conflict, ambiguity, novelty

5. Topical reasoning emphasizes that rhetoric must be suited to:

   a. people who are capable of being influenced and capable of bringing about change
   b. situations in which there is no controlling exigence
   c. the rhetor, the audience, the subject matter, and the situation
   d. situations that call for bilateral communication

Matching

Answers may be used more than once.

1. forensic (b)	a. The president gives a Memorial Day speech honoring American military heroes.
2. deliberative (d, e)	
	b. At a university judiciary hearing, a student makes a statement about why she did not violate the student code of conduct.
3. epideictic (a, c)	
4. inventional	c. In a community service awards ceremony, a speaker praises the volunteer of the year.
5. topical	
	d. A CEO of a large company appears before a congressional committee considering new regulatory measures.
	e. MTV hosts a town hall meeting to discuss race relations.

Short Answer

Explain and provide an example of each of the following statements.

1. Problematic situations are marked by conflict.
2. Problematic situations are marked by novelty.

3. Problematic topics are marked by ambiguity.

4. Topoi are contentless.

5. Topoi are heuristic.

℘
Discussion Prompts

- Ask students to view on their own or in class a prominent recent address. Which genre of speech best characterizes this address? What is your contextual and textual evidence for making this classification? Are elements from other genres present in the speech? What are they? Could this speech be classified differently? Are Aristotle's genres mutually exclusive or can mixed forms appear? Does the classification of genre pre-exist the speech? Is his scheme still useful for categorizing contemporary discourse?

- In groups, ask students to generate speaking ideas about a current public issue (e.g., photo radar, racial profiling, Internet pornography) using conventional brainstorming techniques. Next, have them generate ideas systematically using the three topical systems. Compare and contrast the lists generated with each round. What ideas appeared in more than one round? What ideas were unique to each technique? How does this exercise illustrate that rhetoric is a creative process?

- Have students find newspapers from different parts of the state or nation that are culturally different (rural/urban, wealthy/poor, commercial/agricultural, industrial/technological, northern/southern, etc.) What are the different material topics employed in each news source? What types of audiences are implied by the topics? What types of communities are implied by the topic? What community values can you infer from the topics introduced? What topics appear in both sources? What common values can you infer?

- Topoi are not only useful in generating ideas for what can be said, but can also be used for generating ideas about what's *not* being said in a public discussion. For their case study, have students use the topoi to generate sayables for their issue. (It might also be useful for students to try this exercise on each other's topics, as a way to generate fresh insight and creativity.) Compare the list with the topics present in the public communication about the topic. What is not being said? Why not? Does this reflect how the problem is defined by different publics? Does this reflect different owners' (and disowners') interests? If the problem were defined differently, might these ideas be introduced? What are the consequences of these "unsayables" being absent from public discussion? Should they be introduced? How?

❧ 7 ❧

Using Good Reasons to Persuade

❧
Key Concepts

- **Logos** is argument based on good reasons. Aristotle identified two modes of proof, or argument: **internal** (artistic) and **external** (non-artistic).
- Rhetoric is concerned with developing internal arguments using two methods of proof: **paradigms** (also called **examples**) that follow **inductive** reasoning patterns and **enthymemes** that follow **deductive** reasoning patterns.
- Although inductive reasoning typically proceeds from particular to general, argument by paradigm proceeds from **particular to particular**, linking **parallel cases**.
- An **enthymeme** (or **rhetorical syllogism**) is a truncated syllogism, or one with either a premise or conclusion left unexpressed. Enthymemes must feature **common ground** and a **linking premise**. Because the audience "fills in" the unexpressed part, enthymemes are **co-constructed** by speaker and audience.
- A **case** consists of the overall management of evidence and reasoning to support a proposition.
- **Stasis** occurs when contrary arguments clash and are brought to a standstill. Stasis produces an **issue**, or the clash of ideas that differ about the same thing. From this issue arises a **question** to be decided.

- **Issues** can ban be classified as: **conjectural** (an issue of fact), **definitional** (an issue of naming), **qualitative** (an issue of causes and mitigating circumstances), or **translative** (an issue of procedure).
- Logos is necessary in both public and private settings. In everyday interaction we often offer **accounts**, or explanations of our thoughts and deeds when our actions are called into question. Accounts can be of two types: **justifications** and **excuses**.

❧

Test Items

True or False

1. Rhetoric is best suited to develop external (non-artistic) arguments. (F)
2. You can never use too many examples. (F)
3. Inductive arguments proceed from particular to general. (T)
4. Arguments by paradigm proceed from particular to particular. (T)
5. A justification is an account in which one accepts responsibility. (T)

Multiple Choice

1. Stasis refers to:
   a. a logical argument
   b. the point at which arguments clash
   c. the link between premise and conclusion
   d. an issue of conjecture

2. Enthymemes:
   a. are a necessary part of every rhetorical appeal
   b. demonstrate that the rhetor has conducted an audience analysis
   c. are arguments in which the audience supplies the missing part
   d. all of the above

3. Issues can arise due to differences of:
   a. fact
   b. definition
   c. procedure
   d. all of the above

4. Imagine you are asking your professor for permission not to take the final exam for this class. Which internal (artistic) proof should you use?

   a. a copy of your final exam schedule

   b. your university's final exam scheduling policy

   c. examples of your previous work in the class, indicating your mastery of course material

   d. all of the above

5. An account is:

   a. an explanation of our actions when they are called into question

   b. useful only in forensic speaking situations

   c. an acceptance of responsibility for a situation

   d. an appeal to a higher authority

Matching

1. conjectural issue (f)	a. Are any rights or procedures violated?
2. translative issue (a)	b. Who is going to do something about it?
3. definitional issue (d)	c. What is the nature of the act?
4. qualitative issue (c)	d. What shall we call it?
5. operational definition (e)	e. How does it work?
	f. What happened?

Short Answer

Define and provide an example of each of the following types of account.

1. condemnation of the condemners

2. denial of injury

3. appeal to loyalties

4. appeal to accidents

5. scapegoating

Discussion Prompts

• Choose a landmark Supreme Court case that has easily identifiable stasis points. First Amendment cases work well. (Alternatively, you could view an excerpt from a television or film courtroom drama.) What is the stasis point? What is the issue before the court? Is it an issue of fact, definition, quality, or procedure? What question(s) must the judge or jury answer? How does each side present its case? Identify external proofs, internal proofs, enthymemes, examples, accounts, excuses, and justifications used to support each case. Which side prevailed in the case? How might the defeated side have used logos to improve its case?

- We use logos in our everyday lives. Ask students to think of occasions when they have had to give accounts of their actions. Did you offer justifications or excuses? What types of justifications or excuses did you use? Did you defend your actions successfully? If unsuccessful, would choosing a different type of account to frame your actions have been more persuasive? Why/why not? Do you consider your account an ethical use of logos? Why/why not?

- Ask students to bring to class a copy of the daily campus or local paper. Divide students into groups to examine news, editorial, human interest, and advertising content. Ask each group to identify the different forms of logos being used and share with the class.

- Ask students to bring in opinion and editorial items from various news media. Identify the enthymemes and unpack the missing part. What do these enthymemes assume that the audience will believe or value? Do you, as an audience member, agree with the missing part (i.e., has the author made correct assumptions about you)?

- Ask students to identify the stasis point of the local controversy they are investigating for their case study. What is the issue that arises? What type of issue is it? How are the different techniques of logos used in discourses among the disputants?

- For the case study, ask students to select a representative piece of discourse (mission statement, speech, editorial, leaflet, etc.) for each different group vying for ownership. Analyze each piece of discourse separately to identify the enthymemes, examples, and accounts offered. What does each imply about the audience or publics it is addressing? Then, compare your analyses. Do they rely on common assumptions about the audience? Is the audience being asked to supply similar premises or to identify with similar examples or similar accounts? What are the points of difference? Do these differences relate to the overall stasis point of the controversy? How do these points of commonality and difference suggest potential resolutions to the public problem?

∞ 8 ∞

Persuasiveness of Character

∞
Key Concepts

- In addition to good reasons, rhetorical appeals can be based on ethos. Ethos is not a personal trait, but a **social construct**. **Ethos** is an interpretation that is the product of speaker-audience interaction.

- Ethos is **dynamic** because it is developed through talk. Ethos is a **caused response** because it is a product of a speaker's choices.

- The ancient Greeks assessed good character in terms of **excellence** and **practical wisdom**.

- Audiences consider three types of habits when assessing ethos: **mental habits** (intelligence), **moral habits** (trustworthiness), and **emotional habits** (goodwill).

- Whereas ethos focuses on the perceptions of the speaker caused by her rhetoric, **ethical appeals** focus on the issues raised (or suppressed) and the quality of arguments addressed to them.

- Guidelines for evaluating the ethics of a rhetorical appeal:

  —The speaker uses no device of persuasion that he could not in principle permit others to use on him (Johnstone's **bilateral argument**).

  —The speaker seeks mutual agreement with his audience (Yoos's **A factor**).

  —The speaker recognizes the rational autonomy of his audience (Yoos's **R factor**).

—The speaker recognizes the equality of the listener with himself (Yoos's **E factor**).

—The speaker recognizes that the ends of the audience have an intrinsic value for him (Yoos's **V factor**).

℘
Test Items

True or False

1. A strong ethos means that the speaker legitimately possesses certain attributes of character. (F)

2. Ethos is an interpretation. (T)

3. Ethical appeals focus on the ethics of a person's views. (F)

4. Ethos is a result of the choices a speaker makes about what to include and exclude in her speech. (T)

5. Rhetorical practices are unethical because rhetoric seeks endorsement of partisan opinion, not truth. (F)

Multiple Choice

1. Ethos is developed:
   a. prior to the message
   b. during the message
   c. after the message
   d. regardless of message

2. It is important to assess ethos carefully because:
   a. we tend to trust speakers with whom we identify
   b. first impressions are the only impressions that matter
   c. when all else is equal, we tend to affirm the views of speakers we hold in high esteem
   d. unethical speakers are hard to detect

3. When we assess ethos in terms of a speaker's emotional habits, we should primarily consider:
   a. the speaker's ability to show emotion in a speech
   b. the speaker's intelligence and mastery of the topic
   c. the speaker's past reputation
   d. the speaker's disposition toward the audience

4. Public virtues such as justice, temperance, magnanimity, and prudence are considered when assessing:

a. moral habits

b. authority

c. source credibility

d. emotional habits

5. When critics note that President George W. Bush received only average grades in college, they are questioning his:

a. emotional habits

b. moral habits

c. mental habits

d. intellectual habits

Matching

1. emotional habits (a)   a. goodwill

2. excellence (f)   b. eudaimonia

3. mental habits (e)   c. phronêsis

4. practical wisdom (c)   d. trustworthiness

5. moral habits (d)   e. intelligence

                               f. arête

Short Answer

How is each of the following concepts used to assess the ethics of a rhetorical appeal?

1. bilateral argument

2. A factor

3. R factor

4. E factor

5. V factor

Discussion Prompts

• Aristotle considered ethos to be the most powerful type of artistic proof. Ask students to consider the following statement: "All else being equal, ethos carries the day." Do you believe this is still as true today as it was in ancient Greece? Why do you think this is so (or not so)? Can you think of recent examples when this is not the case? What are the merits of considering ethos as a tiebreaker? What are the problems with considering ethos as a tiebreaker? If not ethos, what else should carry the day?

- White House and congressional Web sites routinely post the texts of major addresses. Ask students to visit a site and select a text suitable for a rhetorical analysis of ethos. How are moral, mental, and emotional habits displayed? What is the textual evidence for your interpretations of the speaker's habits? Using the guidelines for evaluating the ethics of rhetorical appeals, assess the speaker. What recommendations would you make to bolster the speaker's ethos?

- View the August 17, 1998, address of President Bill Clinton following his grand jury testimony about his relationship with Monica Lewinsky ("The Map Room Address"). What was the rhetorical situation of this speech (identify exigence, audience(s), constraints)? Did Clinton provide a fitting response? Is the fitness of his response tied to the ethos he constructs in this speech? For which of his audiences is his ethos most in jeopardy? How does he display (or fail to display) mental, moral, and emotional habits; excellence and wisdom? Evaluate Clinton's address using the guidelines for assessing ethics. How does he live up to (or fail live up to) these guidelines? What specific textual features lead you to your conclusion? If you were advising the president on ethos that night, what would you have recommended he do differently in this speech?

- In the days and weeks following the attacks on the World Trade Center and the Pentagon, the nation witnessed the transformation of ethos of two prominent national figures: President George W. Bush and New York Mayor Rudolph Giuliani. What were typical impressions of Giuliani and Bush before September 11, 2001? How did these interpretations of ethos change in the aftermath of the attacks? What did Bush and Giuliani say and do to effect these interpretations? What did audiences need to hear from their leaders at this time? Did audience expectations play a role in how we interpreted ethos? Did the rhetorical situation play a role in how we interpreted ethos? How does this example inform your understanding of ethos as a social construct rather than a personal trait?

- For the case study, ask students to identify the leading spokespersons for their public issue. Examine representative discourses of each spokesperson and make an assessment of ethos using the concepts and guidelines presented in this chapter and specific evidence from the texts. Then, if possible, have students arrange to interview each person in order to learn more about the issue and more about the ethos of the rhetor. Record the interview (with permission). Conduct a second analysis of ethos on the interview data. Did your perception of ethos change as a result of this one-on-one interaction? Discuss influences of the rhetorical situation and of the rhetor's choices on your interpretations of ethos.

❧ 9 ❧

The Passions

❧
Key Concepts

- In addition to good reasons (logos) and interpretations of character (ethos), rhetoric involves the audience's emotional engagement, or **pathos**. **Pathos** refers to the self-evoking aspects of our total response to the arguments brought before us for our active consideration.

- Emotions are not things or states, they are expressions of **self-involving judgments**, or experiences of seeing oneself as the type of person who exhibits certain behavior when confronted by a specific object of experience. They can be expressed as a **practical syllogism**.

- Emotional judgments are **normative**, **unique** to a given case, **dependent on language**, and experienced in **eventful** ways.

- Emotions feature a **referent** (object of experience), a **feeling** (self-involving judgment), and a projection of the **future** (goal-oriented).

- Each culture is characterized by typical emotional response patterns. The **basic emotions** available are ones that members of a culture may provide by virtue of their acculturation. More important than knowing the basic emotions, however, is knowing the ways in which a given audience responds to typical experiences.

‹≈

Test Items

True or False

1. Ethos refers to an audience's emotional engagement. (F)
2. Basic emotions are culturally specific. (T)
3. Emotions are products of interpretations. (T)
4. When a speaker evokes pathos, we should question his ethics. (F)
5. Rhetoric cannot avoid engaging our emotions. (T)

Multiple Choice

1. From a rhetorical perspective, emotions are:
   a. patterns of response
   b. inflicted upon us from the outside
   c. qualities we possess
   d. general feelings

2. Emotions are thoughts with respect to a referent. This means that:
   a. emotions are bound by culture
   b. emotions are oriented toward a particular goal
   c. emotions are self-involving judgments
   d. emotions are tied to objects of experience

3. All of the following are features of emotions **except**:
   a. telic
   b. normative
   c. generalized
   d. eventful

4. Emotional responses are conditioned by our:
   a. language
   b. reason
   c. character
   d. intellect

5. Practical syllogisms:
   a. link cultural values with basic response patterns
   b. put an object of experience in relation to the self
   c. focus on the logic of a message
   d. link our feelings to our goals

Matching

1. ethos (c)   a. audience-involved judgments
2. pathos (d)   b. put an object in relation to the self
3. logos (f)   c. source-involved judgments
4. practical syllogisms (b)   d. self-involved judgments
5. rhetorical syllogisms (e)   e. enthymemes
                                                    f. subject-involved judgments

Short Answer

Explain and provide an example of each of the following statements.

1. Emotions are normative.
2. Emotions are unique.
3. Emotions depend on language.
4. Emotions are eventful.
5. Emotions are culturally specific.

ح

Discussion Prompts

- Hauser argues that when considering pathos, we need to determine whether our feelings are appropriate for making wise decisions. Ask students to think of two rhetorical events they have experienced in which their emotions were strongly engaged. One should be an event in which their emotional response might be considered as appropriate, whereas the other should be considered inappropriate. How did you come to the conclusion that your emotional response was either appropriate or inappropriate? What strategies did the speaker (or your interlocutor) use to elicit an emotional response? How do we know that the emotions evoked by a rhetor are appropriate? Who makes this determination? How did the ways in which the speaker invoked pathos influence your interpretations of ethos?

- Ask students to select any sort of print flyer that seeks to change behavior, such as investing money, supporting a social cause, practicing safe sex, volunteering, quitting smoking, etc. In class, analyze the flyer. How is pathos operating as a rhetorical appeal? What emotions does the flyer intend to invoke? What is the specific evidence for your claim? The flyer asks for a particular sort of emotional response from its audience. How can this response be rendered in the form of a practical syllogism? Have the creators of the flyer used pathos responsibly? Does it attempt to engage emotions in an ethically acceptable way? Why or why not?

- Late last night, two university students were violently assaulted on campus. Today, rumors are spreading that the assault was a racially motivated "hate crime." As president of student government, you have been asked to write an editorial about the incident for publication in tomorrow's campus newspaper. You sense that emotions are running high on campus, and you want to draw on these emotions in ways that are both appropriate and responsible. Write your editorial. Reflect on your rhetorical choices, specifically with regard to pathos. What was your telos? How did you make decisions to involve emotions in appropriate and responsible ways?

- View a speech appropriate for a study in pathos (e.g., Oprah Winfrey's remarks at the New York City Prayer Service in Yankee Stadium, 9/23/01; President George W. Bush, "Freedom and Fear are at War," 9/20/01; Elizabeth Glaser's speech to the Democratic National Convention, 7/14/92; Malcolm X's "The Ballot or the Bullet," 4/3/64). Initiate a discussion of how pathos is developed in the speech. What are some of the emotions that are aroused? Are some of these emotions basic emotions? What emotions are not included in Aristotle's and Solomon's inventories? How does the speaker arouse specific emotions? Ground your claims with specific textual evidence.

- For the case study, ask students to identify discourses appropriate for a study in pathos. Analyze how pathos is developed in the discourses. Compare and contrast how pathos is developed by different owners of the issue. What are the consequences of their respective uses of pathos for rendering public judgment on this issue?

∾ 10 ∾

Narrative

∾
Key Concepts

- **Narratives** are stories that organize and give meanings to rhetorical situations and suggest appropriate ways to respond. **Narrative framing** is an act of rhetorical invention that provides a context for ordering the elements of an episode and interpreting its meaning.

- Narratives have distinctive structural features. A **plot** is a sequence of occurrences that relate to one another in a meaningful whole. Sequence helps us to determine the meaning of the story through its **episodic dimension** (chronology) and **configural operation** (patterning).

- Narratives help to define the **nomos** (normative universe) of a culture. **Historicity** refers to our sense of being part of our cultural history, of having a tradition that exerts an important defining force on our beliefs and values as a member of our culture.

- Narrative reasoning involves **narrative quest**, or a search for closure in a story.

- Narratives make **public moral arguments**. They contribute to a community's public memory.

- **Narrative probability** refers to the coherence of the story. Narrative probability can be assessed by **argumentative** or **structural coherence** (Is the story internally consistent?), **material coherence** (How does it stand in relation to other stories and discourses?), and **characterological coherence** (Are the people of the story acting in characteristic ways?).

- **Narrative fidelity** refers to the extent to which the story rings true with the stories that audience members have known to be true in their lives.
- Narrators don't just tell a story—they have voice. **Voice** refers to the presentational quality of a narrative; it provides orientation through its point of view. We can interpret narrative voice as **reliable** or **unreliable**.

℘
Test Items

True or False

1. We make sense of our world primarily through narratives. (T)
2. A narrator is the author of a story. (F)
3. Narratives are valid forms of public moral argument. (T)
4. Historicity is constituted by a culture's narratives. (T)
5. Audiences primarily judge public arguments by logical validity. (F)

Multiple Choice

1. Narratives:
   a. involve the audience in patterns of perception
   b. help to organize experience
   c. are rhetorical inventions
   d. all of the above

2. The extent to which a story rings true with the audience's experience is called:
   a. narrative probability
   b. narrative paradigm
   c. narrative fidelity
   d. narrative quest

3. A narrative quest:
   a. appeals to the audience's sense of historicity
   b. seeks closure by eliminating gaps
   c. orders the elements of a story into a coherent sequence
   d. involves a hero and some obstacle to be overcome

4. Voice refers to:

    a. the presentational quality of a narrative

    b. the representational quality of a narrative

    c. the characterological quality of a narrative

    d. the historical fidelity of a narrative

5. _____ assumes that humans are valuing as much as reasoning creatures.

    a. The canon of invention

    b. A concept of historicity

    c. Narrative framing

    d. The narrative paradigm

Matching

1. material coherence (b)	a. Does the story fit with my experience?
2. characterological coherence (f)	b. Have counterarguments been omitted?
	c. What is the moral of the story?
3. narrative quest (d)	d. How does the story end?
4. narrative fidelity (a)	e. Is the story internally consistent?
5. structural coherence (e)	f. Are the people of the story acting in characteristic ways?

Short Answer

Define and provide an example of each of the following concepts.

1. narrative framing

2. plot

3. voice

4. historicity

5. public memory

႙

Discussion Prompts

- Ask students to recall typical family, organizational, or institutional stories, the types that get told and retold at social gatherings, to new members, and the like. What is the basic plot of the story? Does the narrative shift with each telling? Does the meaning of the narrative change with the voice of the narrator? How does this story convey the group's values? Recalling chapter 2, how does the narrative transmit norms and traditions? Does the narrative invite criticism of norms and values?

- Engage students in an analysis and discussion of the following story. (See J. Martin, M. J. Feldman, and S. Sitkin, "The Uniqueness Paradox in Organizational Stories," *Administrative Science Quarterly* 28 (1983): 438–53, and Dennis K. Mumby, "The Political Function of Narrative in Organizations," *Communication Monographs* 54 (1987): 113–127.)

  Newcomers at IBM eventually hear a story about Thomas Watson, Jr., former chairman of the board. One day, Watson is challenged by a supervisor, a twenty-two-year-old bride weighing ninety pounds whose husband had been sent overseas and who, in consequence, had been given a job until his return. . . . The young woman, Lucille Burger, was obliged to make certain that people entering security areas wore the correct, clear identification.

  Surrounded by his usual entourage of white-shirted men, Watson approached the doorway to an area where she was on guard, wearing an orange badge acceptable elsewhere in the plant, but not a green badge, which alone permitted entrance at her door. "I was trembling in my uniform, which was far too big," she recalled. "It hid my shakes, but not my voice. 'I'm sorry,' I said to him. I knew who he was all right. 'You cannot enter. Your admittance is not recognized.' That's what we were supposed to say."

  The men accompanying Watson were stricken; the moment had unpredictable possibilities. "Don't you know who he is?" someone hissed. Watson raised his hand for silence, while one of the party strode off and returned with the appropriate badge.

- For the case study, ask students to identify narratives associated with their issue. Analyze how narratives are developed in the discourse. How do the narratives frame the issue? Identify plot, voice, narrative quest, etc. Do they meet the standards of narrative probability and narrative fidelity? How do the narratives engage historicity? How do they contribute to the construction of public memory? How are they functioning as public moral arguments about this issue?

❧ 11 ❧

Acting with Language

❧
Key Concepts

- Classical rhetoric focuses on persuasion, whereas contemporary rhetoric focuses on **identification**.

- **Motion** refers to the nonsymbolic or extrasymbolic operations of nature. **Action** refers to the type of behavior that becomes possible with the use of symbols.

- Humans act with language. **Speech act theory** holds that each utterance has three components: what is said (**locution**); what is done in the saying (**illocution**), and the psychological impact of what was said (**perlocution**).

- Burke's **Dramatism** holds that we manage symbols to coordinate social action—symbols act dynamically to shape our world. Dramatism rests upon Burke's definition of the human as the symbol-using (misusing) animal, inventor (or invented by) the negative, separated from his natural condition by instruments of his own making, goaded by a spirit of hierarchy, and rotten with perfection.

- A rhetorical perspective takes a **presentational** view of reality. A presentational view holds that when we use symbols, we create meanings with others; that symbols organize and project a world; and that communication stems from its situated context.

- As a model, **Dramatism** examines the ways in which we use language in the format of dramatic action. The **dramatic pentad** consists of **act** (what was done), **scene** (where the act occurred), **agent** (who performed the act), **agency** (the means of acting), and **pur-**

pose (the goal of the act). **Attitude** (a disposition or "incipient action") rounds out the pentad.

- We act according to **motives**. Rhetorically understood, motives are social—not psychological—constructs. Motives are "shorthand for situations" and are present in our language. Through the process of socialization, we learn **vocabularies of motives**, which provide group identity and an orientation toward the world.

- Rhetoric functions to produce **identification**, where we find that our ways are like another's; symbolically, we are one in terms of a shared principle (**consubstantiality**). As a **dialectical** term, identification implies its opposite, **division**. Rhetoric also functions to compensate for division. **Misidentification** occurs when we falsely believe our ways and another's are one.

- Vocabularies of motives provide conceptual patterns for interpreting reality; these patterns are selective. A vocabulary of motives acts as a **terministic screen**, emphasizing some aspects of experience and ignoring others.

∞
Test Items

True or False
1. There can be motion without action. (T)
2. There can be action without motion. (F)
3. Action is not reducible to terms of motion. (T)
4. Dramatism holds that language is a representational system. (F)
5. An attitude is an incipient act. (T)

Multiple Choice
1. Classical rhetoric emphasizes ___ while contemporary rhetoric emphasizes _____.
   a. perception, identification
   b. identification, persuasion
   c. identification, opinion
   d. persuasion, identification

2. Identification implies:
   a. dialectic
   b. action
   c. attitude
   d. division

3. When Burke says that humans are "inventors of the negative," he means:

  a. we make factual choices about the true and false

  b. we make moral choices

  c. we are striving for perfection

  d. we are prone to misidentification

4. According to Burke, which of the following is *not* true:

  a. rhetoric is an enhancement of language

  b. rhetoric is a use of language

  c. rhetoric is directed to symbol-using animals

  d. rhetoric is a means of inducing cooperation

5. Motives are:

  a. incipient acts

  b. acting with language

  c. shorthand terms for situations

  d. psychological attitudes

Matching

Match the elements of the dramatic pentad with features of President Bill Clinton's "Map Room Address" about his relationship with Monica Lewinsky (8/17/98).

1. act (c)

2. scene (a)

3. agent (f)

4. agency (e)

5. purpose (d)

a. "a politically inspired lawsuit which has since been dismissed" and an independent counsel investigation which is "itself under investigation"

b. Kenneth Starr

c. "I misled people": the court, the public, my family

d. "a desire to protect myself from the embarrassment of my own conduct" and "protecting my family"

e. "While my answers were legally accurate, I did not volunteer information" and "my silence on this matter"

f. Bill Clinton

Short Answer

Define and provide an example of each of the following concepts.

1. identification
2. misidentification
3. division
4. presentational view of communication
5. vocabulary of motives

୬

Discussion Prompts

- Ask students to bring in examples of print advertisements that appear to be fostering identification (ads in which the product is not explicitly featured work well). Analyze the ads in class. What symbolic resources promote identification (and division)? How do these resources interact with larger vocabularies of motives?

- Identification is a powerful political campaign strategy. View several political campaign ads in class (campaign films work well too). How does the candidate attempt to establish identification with different audiences? What divisions are created in the process? How does the candidate establish division with his opponents? What do these identification and division strategies imply about the candidate's view of his or her audiences? How do they intersect with larger vocabularies of motives? Do the ads invite misidentification?

- Ask students to identify prevalent contemporary vocabularies of motives (e.g., capitalism, globalism, environmentalism, feminism, technological progress, fundamentalism, liberalism, conservatism, etc.). Working in groups, have students brainstorm the vocabulary. What ideas, terms, and concepts are associated with the vocabulary? Where and how is this vocabulary expressed? What motives are at work in the vocabulary? How does the vocabulary work as a terministic screen? How does it project a world?

- In class, view or read the text of a speech suitable for pentadic criticism. Edward Kennedy's "Chappaquiddick" address is a classic (7/25/69). Consider using a text you have used previously in the semester, so that students can get a new angle on the text, and to encourage discussion about old and new rhetoric, persuasion, and identification. Identify the elements of the pentad as evidenced in Kennedy's speech. From his version of the drama, what can we infer about motives? Could the dramatic elements have been named differently (i.e., how might an opponent script the drama)? What motives could be inferred from an alternate presentation?

- For the case study, ask students to identify the vocabularies of motives associated their issue. Analyze how these vocabularies are developed in the public discourse about the issue. How do they operate as terministic screens? How do they promote identification and division? How do these vocabularies promote or inhibit social cooperation?

♔ 12 ♔

Experiencing Meaning in Rhetoric

♔
Key Concepts

- The meaning of language depends on its use. **Meaning** is the significance of an utterance as it emerges from a context of usage and the perceptions that it invites. **Perception** is the interpretive awareness of a referent.

- Rhetoric produces meaning as **situated utterances**; meaning is specific to particular issues and audiences or publics.

- Language usage is experientially based. The ways in which we understand our world are conditioned by the interactions we have with our physical environment (**ontological** experiences and cultural orientation).

- Perceptual patterns emerge from contexts of experience. These patterns provide us with a stock of common assumptions, values, expectations, and motives that make it possible for us to share our perceptions with others.

- Language use contains inherent frameworks for conceptualizing what we experience. These frames (**schemas**) organize experience in a particular way.

- Meaning emerges from the interaction among symbols within their context of use. The **context theorem of meaning** holds that words are successfully meaningful in the contexts insofar as they animate and are animated.

55

- Symbols act to create meaning **within an utterance**. Grammar, vocabulary and imagery can imbue meaning in significant ways.

- Symbols act to create meaning within **extended verbal utterances**. Larger frameworks such as a paragraph, an argument, and an entire work help to illuminate and modify meanings.

- Symbols act to create meaning within **external contexts** (e.g., rhetorical situation).

- According to Richards, **metaphors** are not merely stylistic devices, they are cornerstones of meaning and thought. **Metaphoric statements** rely on metaphors for their essential meaning—no literal equivalent can be used without destroying the essential meaning of the statement.

- In a metaphor, the salient term is called a **focus**, while the **frame** consists of the literal portion of the utterance. Frame and focus interplay to create their unique meaning.

- Metaphor develops meaning by talking about one thing (**principal subject**) in terms of another (**subsidiary subject**).

- A **system of associated commonplaces** consists of the standard beliefs shared by members of the same speech community when they use a term literally.

- Novel metaphors have two features: emphasis and resonance. **Emphasis** refers to the degree to which the focus is essential for the meaning of the metaphor. **Resonance** refers to the number of implications we can draw from the interplay between the principal subject and the subsidiary subject.

- Metaphors generate new information, or a body of implications (**the implicative complex**) that restructures our perceptions of reality.

ॐ
Test Items

True or False

1. Meaning is the interpretive awareness of a referent. (F)
2. Meanings are in the dictionary. (F)
3. Meaning can be divorced from action. (F)
4. Metaphoric statements invite substitution of terms. (F)
5. Novel metaphors feature emphasis and resonance. (T)

Multiple Choice

1. According to the context theorem of meaning:

   a. meaning is a property of the words themselves

   b. meanings depend on the context of usage

   c. metaphoric implications structure our perception of reality

   d. each word has a proper meaning

2. Which of the following is not one of the four propositions of meaning?

   a. meaning emerges from the denotation of words across contexts

   b. the only way we can know the meaning of words is in the context of interaction

   c. language contains inherent frameworks for conceptualizing what we experience

   d. language is experientially based

3. Symbols act to create meaning:

   a. within an utterance

   b. within extended verbal utterances

   c. within external contexts

   d. all of the above

4. One test of a metaphor's strength refers to the degree to which the meaning of a statement would change if the focus changed. This is called:

   a. emphasis

   b. resonance

   c. ontology

   d. situated utterance

5. In the metaphor, "this company is one big family," the term "family" is:

   a. the principal subject

   b. the subsidiary subject

   c. the resonant subject

   d. the literal subject

Matching

1. focus (a)   a. the salient term of a metaphor
2. frame (e)   b. the thing talked about in a metaphor
3. schema (f)   c. the term applied in a metaphor
4. principal subject (b)   d. the implication of a metaphor
5. subsidiary subject (c)   e. the literal portion of a metaphor
                                 f. a framework of experience

Short Answer

Define each of the following terms.

1. mediation model
2. system of associated commonplaces
3. context theorem of meaning
4. implicative context
5. metaphoric statement

❧
Discussion Prompts

• Ask students to brainstorm some common metaphors used to portray aspects of contemporary life (e.g., rat race, time is money, melting pot/mosaic, war on drugs, invisible hand of the market). What aspects of the social do these metaphors highlight? Select one metaphor to unpack. How did this metaphor develop? Identify the focus, frame, principal subject, and subsidiary subject. Evaluate emphasis and resonance. How do the terms interact to generate meaning? Work out the implicative context of the metaphor. What is the perception of reality encouraged by the metaphor? Replace the subsidiary subject with another term. How does the new metaphor interact to generate new meaning?

• In class, view or read a rhetorical text rich with metaphors (e.g., Martin Luther King's "I Have a Dream" is a classic; also recommended is India's Prime Minister Jawaharlal Nehru's eulogy for Mohandas Gandhi, 2/2/48; song lyrics can work well). Identify the dominant metaphors. Identify the focus, frame, principal subject, and subsidiary subject. Evaluate emphasis and resonance. How do the terms interact to generate meaning? How are these metaphors developed within an utterance (grammar, vocabulary, imagery)? How are they developed within extended verbal utterances? How are they developed within external contexts? What meanings are generated in each of these contexts? What are the systems of associated commonplaces with the terms? Work out the implicative complex. What interpretations of reality are encouraged by these metaphors? How are metaphors used to establish identification?

- Organizational life is often represented metaphorically (e.g., machine, family, organism, brain, culture, web, political system; See Gareth Morgan, *Images of Organization*, 2nd ed. Thousand Oaks, CA: Sage, 1997). How did these metaphors develop? What are their systems of associated commonplaces? What aspects of organizational life do they highlight? What aspects do they obscure? How do they work as schemas or frameworks of experience? How do they give meaning to organizational life? How might these metaphors influence the thought and conduct of organizational members?

- Have students read Friedrich Nietzsche's *On Truth and Lie in an Extra-Moral Sense* (1879) or consider the following excerpt:

    "What, then, is truth? A mobile army of metaphors, metonyms, and anthropomorphisms—in short, a sum of human relations which have been enhanced, transposed, and embellished poetically and rhetorically, and which after long use seem firm, canonical, and obligatory to people: truths are illusions about which one has forgotten that this is what they are; metaphors which are worn out and without sensuous power; coins which have lost their pictures and now matter as metal, no longer as coins."

    Relate to the ideas discussed in chapter 12. What is Nietzsche saying about meaning and truth? How does he use metaphor to make his case? Could he have used anything but metaphor to make his case?

- For the case study, ask students to identify and analyze the metaphors employed in the public discussion of their issue. How do they create meaning and organize perception about the issue? How do they work across contexts and draw from systems of associated commonplaces? Work out the implicative complex. What interpretations of reality are encouraged by these metaphors?

✐ 13 ✐

Rhetorical Form
as Strategy

✐
Key Concepts

- Rhetoric is a mode of **strategic action**, discourse devised for a particular situation in order to achieve a goal.

- Structures are basic to perception. Six basic patterns of human perception are: edging, rhythm, association, classification, abstraction, and hierarchy.

- The five principles of **structure in the large** are: (1) all human perception is selective perception, (2) our perception of reality requires some structure, (3) the structures we perceive have a variety of forms, (4) all of our experiences have structure or form, and (5) because experience is tied to structure, changes in structure lead to changes of experience.

- All **structures** invite a particular expectation of patterned development and completion. Rhetorical **forms** encourage the anticipation of an outcome, and if properly developed, satisfy this anticipation.

- Structures are **strategic** in that they influence how we respond to messages.

- Structures reveal **motives**; they adopt certain strategies for sizing up a situation.

- **Associational clusters** are terms and ideas that congregate and act together. They tell us "what goes with what" for a speaker and what sorts of associations he wants the audience to make.

- Burke identified five major rhetorical forms. **Syllogistic progression** is a form of argument in which each premise logically leads to the next. Given certain premises, others must follow. **Qualitative progression** is when the presence of one quality prepares us for another. **Repetitive form** occurs when we consistently maintain a principle by presenting it in different ways. **Conventional form** is a culturally recognizable form. Certain situations lead us to expect typical forms. **Minor forms** are expressive or stylistic devices; figures of speech.

- Hariman identified forms of political style, or "coherent repertoire[s] of rhetorical conventions depending on aesthetic reactions for political effect." The **realist style** separates power and artistic discourse. Verbal artistry is downplayed in favor of a plain style of talk. The **courtly style** places emphasis on the proximity of people in relation to the center of political power. Status is a function of proximity to power. The **republican style** emphasizes the merits of discussion and deliberation in forging public agreement. Status is a function of skill and civic virtue. The **bureaucratic style** emphasizes codified, rational rules and procedures. Written communication is more valued than spoken communication.

ళ
Test Items

True or False

1. Structures are strategic. (T)
2. Changes in structure lead to changes of experience. (T)
3. Aesthetics play no role in politics. (F)
4. Metaphors are types of minor forms. (T)
5. Forms are universal; they are not guided by culture. (F)

Multiple Choice

1. Humans perceive the world as:
   a. disorganized chaos
   b. clusters of association
   c. structured patterns
   d. systems of commonplaces

2. Rhetorical structures can help us to reveal a rhetor's:

   a. motives

   b. strategic responses to a situation

   c. understanding of the situation

   d. all of the above

3. Associative clusters are:

   a. congregations of terms that tell us "what goes with what"

   b. repertoires of rhetorical conventions depending on aesthetic re-actions for political effect

   c. structures that encourage anticipation and resolution

   d. sets of principles abstracted from seemingly disparate events

4. According to Gregg, all of the following are basic patterns of per-ception *except*:

   a. association

   b. progression

   c. classification

   d. abstraction

5. The unique feature of rhetorical forms is that:

   a. they apply to only some of our experiences

   b. they are the result of the interaction between two thoughts

   c. they encourage the anticipation and satisfaction of an outcome

   d. all of the above

Matching

1. republican style (d)
2. courtly style (a)
3. realist style (f)
4. bureaucratic style (c)
5. political style (b)

a. "I got backstage at the Galactic con-cert last night!"

b. a repertoire of conventions depending on aesthetic reactions for political effect

c. "Didn't you see the memo?"

d. "I don't believe it. Professor Hauser would never do something like that."

e. "what goes with what"

f. "I'm just telling it like it is."

Short Answer

Define and provide an example for each of the following terms:

1. syllogistic progression
2. qualitative progression
3. repetitive form
4. conventional form
5. minor forms

༄

Discussion Prompts

- Ask students to brainstorm different forms or genres of popular media (e.g., situation comedies, police and courtroom dramas, soap operas, reality programs, documentaries, afternoon talk shows, late night talk shows, local news programs, news magazines, Internet chat rooms, computer games, multi-user domains, Internet shopping outlets, company home pages, etc.). Assign groups of students to observe carefully an instance or two of this form. In class, discuss the different types of forms in detail. Explain in terms of progression and political style, if appropriate. How do structural components shape desired audience perceptions? Have these forms changed over time? What factors led to this transformation? Can specific instances of a genre break form? To what end?

- Give students a simple claim and its antithesis (e.g., survival of the fittest vs. the meek will inherit the earth; the rugged individual vs. it takes a village to raise a child). Ask them to develop how they would forward each of these claims using Burke's five basic forms. How do the different structures convey meanings about these axioms? Do different structures bring different aspects of the principle to light? Considering that you can use the same forms to convey opposing messages, what does that say about structures? What does that say about rhetorical strategy?

- View a selection of political campaign commercials or public service announcements (from television ads, print media, candidate and political action committee Web sites). How do the different candidates employ particular political styles? Do candidates make use of more than one style? What style is common to several candidates? What conclusions can you draw about the candidates? How do these styles imply a candidate's vision of the public? What conclusions can you draw about American political culture in the large?

- Ask students to identify recurring rhetorical situations with which a formal public address is typically associated (e.g., eulogies, commencement speeches, acceptance speeches, apologia, crisis rhetoric, inaugurals, victory and concession speeches, etc.). Do these situations call for different forms of address? What are the typical features of these forms? How do the structures evoke and satisfy a particular audience response? How do forms relate to fitting responses?

- For the case study, ask students to identify the typical forms of discourse employed in the public discussion of their issue. What types of forms are present? Do different owners and publics employ different types of forms? How do the different forms shape their message? How is the audience expected to respond to different forms?

- For the case study, ask students to identify the political styles employed in the public discussion of their issue. What styles are typically used? Do different owners and publics seem to draw from particular repertoires of style? How do these styles shape their message? How is the audience expected to respond to the styles used? Do the styles foster identification and division? How?

❧ 14 ❧

Strategic Forms of
Argument Structures

❧
Key Concepts

- The form of an argument—or **argument structure**—shapes the way it develops; structures function as arguments in themselves.

- Aristotle's **syllogistic structure** is based on deductive logic. We can test the validity of an argument by examining the relationships among its premises. From these relationships, we either can or cannot deduce a conclusion. Syllogistic logic is **field-invariant**: all arguments, regardless of content, are subject to the same rules of inference for drawing conclusions.

- Toulmin's model of **warranted assent** holds that people don't argue syllogistically in practice. The validity of arguments depends on the particular case and context, and thus arguments are **field-dependent**: what counts as valid in one context may not count in another.

- Toulmin's main line of argument consists of **data** (fact and opinion), **warrant** (rationale for inference), and **claim** (conclusion). The force of an argument consists of **backing** (evidence), **rebuttal** (exceptions to the warrant), and **qualifier** (strength of the claim).

- Perelman and Olbrechts-Tyteca hold that the audience determines whether or not an argument works by using schemes of association and dissociation. **Association** brings together separate elements to establish a unity among them. **Dissociation** separates elements that are generally regarded as being unified.

65

- **Associative structures** include quasi-logical arguments and reality-structure arguments. **Quasi-logical arguments** draw from logical form to compel a conclusion. **Reality-structure arguments** draw upon our perceptions of patterns of experience to encourage acceptance of a specific assertion.
- Dramatism holds that dramatic form (e.g., the pentad) influences how arguments develop and are evaluated. Specifically, **scenic** elements invite the audience to perceive arguments in particular ways.

❧

Test Items

True or False

1. Syllogistic form is field-dependent. (F)
2. Scene structures arguments. (T)
3. Quasi-logical arguments are associative structures. (T)
4. Syllogistic structure is based on logical induction. (F)
5. Dissociation calls interpretive patterns into question. (T)

Multiple Choice

1. The Toulmin model holds that valid inferences depend upon:
   a. the specific field of argument
   b. clusters of association
   c. qualifiers about the data
   d. properly worded premises

2. "All men are mortal. Socrates is a man. Therefore, Socrates is mortal." This statement illustrates which argument structure?
   a. enthymeme
   b. syllogism
   c. quasi-logical
   d. reality-structure

3. Reality-structure arguments are:
   a. based on informal logic
   b. based on separating elements thought to be unified
   c. based on our perceptions of patterns of experience
   d. based on inferences drawn from the evidence presented

4. For Perelman and Olbrechts-Tyteca, the test of an argument's validity rests with the:

   a. associative complex

   b. maker of the argument

   c. warrant

   d. audience

5. All of the following are types of reality-structure arguments *except*:

   a. example

   b. probability

   c. analogy

   d. pragmatic

Matching

1. data (a)

2. warrant (d)

3. claim (b)

4. backing (c)

5. qualifier (f)

a. "In the past five years, rents have risen an average of 25%. The average price of a house is 40% above the national average."

b. "City council should look into methods rent control."

c. "People are moving to nearby towns where rents are cheaper."

d. "The people of Boulder need more affordable housing."

e. "Rents are determined by the price people are willing to pay to live here."

f. "The issue is at least worth exploring further."

Short Answer

Define and provide an example for each of the following concepts.

1. syllogistic argument

2. Toulmin's model of argument

3. quasi-logical argument

4. reality-structure argument

5. dissociative argument

ॐ
Discussion Prompts

- Ask students to bring in a copy of the daily student or local newspaper. Have groups of students identify different types of argument structures discussed in this chapter. Identify the elements of the argument. Assess according to the tests of validity appropriate for that type of argument.

- Give students a simple proposition (e.g., the university should ban beer on campus). How would you craft an argument in favor of this proposition using the different argument structures presented in this chapter? Using the same structures, how would you oppose it?

- For the case study, ask students to identify discourses that contain interesting arguments developed by different owners of the issue. Which argument structures are typically employed? Assess the validity of these arguments. What potential counter arguments or rebuttals could be developed? What counterarguments could be made, but are not? Why not?